Light-Years Away

(The Art of Psychic Distance)

Carla Stout

CONTENTS

FROM THE LIGHTHOUSE 5

WORMHOLES, VIVALDI AND IRIS..6

RIDING CLOUDS 7

VIVALDI'S WINTER AND VAN GOGH'S MISTRAL 8

VERMEER'S THE ART OF PAINTING...10

REMOTE FISHING RFV.19..12

JOHN WILLIAMS' DANCE OF WITCHES AND DRACO I...................13

LOOKING GLASS MENAGERIE 16

DAVID GARRETT'S COVER OF NIRVANA'S "TEEN SPIRIT" AND LURE OF
A BLACK STAR 18

SHAKESPEARE'S REVERIES 21

J. S. BACH'S "TOCCATA AND FUGUE" AND THE BLACK SUN 24

DOWN TO EARTH 27

PUCCINI'S "LE VILLI" ACT II: LA TREGENDA" (WITCHES' SABBATH)....28

AND DRACO II 28

REMOTE FISHING RFV.20..31

MOZART'S "REQUIEM" – EXCERPTS (DIES IRAE) AND........................32

THE BELLS AND BEASTS OF NOTRE DAME 32

ORACLES 35

M. WILLIAMS' "CLASSICAL GAS"/D. GARRETT'S "BAROQUE
REINVENTION" AND RUNAWAYS..38

MENDELSSOHN'S "HEBRIDES OVERTURE" AND RAVEN 40

OFF ROAD 43

DARK MATTERS 44

GENESIS OF DEVOLUTION 46

MATTER OF FACT..48

MOZART'S "SYMPHONY NO. 25" ALLEGRO CON BRIO AND FAIRY 49

"PLAINCHANTS" GREGORIAN/ANONYMOUS 4 AND DRUIDS 52

OF BIRDS AND ANGELS 55

HARVEST MOON (PROMPTED BY M. DAVIS' "ROUND MIDNIGHT") 56

BEAUTIES AND BEASTIES 58

SAINT-SAENS' "DANSE MACABRE" AND STARLINGS 59

REMOTE FISHING RFV.21 62

WAGNER'S "SIEGFRIED'S FUNERAL MARCH" AND EULOGY FOR
CIGNUS X-1 63

READING *HAMLET* 65

ORFF'S "CARMINA BURANA-O FORTUNA" AND PULSARS 68

VOLLENWEIDER'S "CAVERNA MAGICA" (1ST TRACK) AND HIKING IN
SICILY 71

EAGLES' "HOTEL CALIFORNIA" AND MARTIAN TERRITORY 74

OLDFIELD'S "TUBULAR BELLS" (1ST TRACK) AND LEONARDO 77

LIGHT-YEARS AWAY PLAYLIST 81

From the Lighthouse

Clouds, black sheep,
stampede toward some
vanishing point while waves
of discontent foment
to meet them. No warning
in skies that grumble.
No place to take cover.
No solace in seagulls.
Even albatross cling
to craggy slippery rocks.

It is my duty to watch
them from some safe
distance amidst surging
ominous clouds and dread.
Yet, there is nothing
I can do to stop this
twist of winds rearing
up out of nowhere.
Nothing to do but log
this far-flung threat.

Up here I could stand
back and paint this riptide
scene. slate, seafoam, black
and blue. But, how do you
paint cold-blooded winds?
How do you gesso despair?
No paint for desolation.
No canvas for decimation.
Yes, I should stand back but,
I cannot travel that distance.

Wormholes, Vivaldi and Iris

Tracings of frost on brittle windows
lend strange matter on a sill-gripping
day. Some are feathers, broad enough
to fan tropic fevers or fires of stars.

Some are toothed leaves, lacings of wood
nymphs. And some, no doubt, are wormholes,
their castings prismatic and anti-material
as the crystals which form them.

If only I could slip inside and slide
from one end, the Ice Age,
to another, a wave of purple iris
and Vivaldi's hot dark matter,

where birds are clocks- - - tick,
tick, flocking away. But somehow,
I get stuck inside, not enough exotic
matter to take me back or ahead,

too much doesn't matter in my blood,
too much gravity in my bed.
I am aloof to shadows on the wall,
because just as quickly shadows warp

to stranger shadows. Imagine us, physicists,
with our linear accelerators building
wormholes from hell to heaven, smirking.
Wait till the poets get their hands on this.

Riding Clouds

How fast/slow silver crosses pass
through blue scrim with white trails of pilgrims,
who pierce cirrus with fervent prayers,
longing to find eternity in mortal shrines,
never heeding wails of wild-eyed soothsayers.
At miles length skeins of clouds bear gentle rains
that fashion rainbows in windows
for lions, tigers, wolves and bears.
When rain dwindles, gray forms yield to blue,
revealing haloed heads, holy and fair.

Further above, clouds skid along where winds whisk strong
and plant vital seeds without heed to flood or drought.
In those times, pilgrims fall on knees to the ground,
their eyes not lifted to thinnest aire and hope,
their eyes, tearing without a sound.
Layers of vapors are traps leaving gaps
between heaven and earth that darken
melancholy minds seized in winter,
never reaching beyond their grasp
to gin from seed the finest fibers of linter.

Witness mysteries in clouds of revealing histories
of daylight moons, aligning and shining
with shrouded suns, spinning slipstreams
of fairy tale stories all caught up
in drafts of fire and ice and unseen dreams.
Closer now, from clutter of trees, clouds
shadow creatures that hover over blackest earth
and forget-me-nots waiting for rain.
We know riding clouds is required for painting
and writing clouds and All that remains.

Vivaldi's Winter and Van Gogh's Mistral

I.
a curtain of slashing, willful
strings *crescendo* from innocence.
unrelenting they stab until the concert
master pulses with paisley plasma
only to be joined again by lesser chairs,
an acute response. feverish, almost mayhem.

> Vincent should have worn his hat,
> his crazed face already a canvas
> gessoed red by the sun, no matter
> for Arles' solar needles. No time to spare- - -
> he weighs down his easel and turns tubes
> of paint to earth, while rays of the sun
> splinter to reveal other stars shining
> as intensely as our own. Untamed,
> his brush takes wild to wheat fields.

II.
senza abbandonare la corda,
without abandoning the strings,
the violin interlude is dawn's
dew on grass. It's rhythmic clock,
a blue heart ticking in plum fields,
marking blush to harvest. But stolen
melodies are spoiled by cheap April showers.

> Finally, here's Roulin, a friend to count on,
> bringing dejeuner for Vincent. Bread, olives,
> lavender honey and flacon of absinthe. Not hungry
> but parched, he feels this heat and reaches
> for absinthe to slake an unquenchable
> thirst. He smiles and wipes his brow.

III.
a *fermata* allows but a brief
pause. minor keys signal
a retreat, the sun, the calm

backing into a stray cloud. fighting
drag of winds, the concert master
pulls on kite strings, on heart's
desire, on abandon. Once again,
tremolo of strings, *agitato.*

> Scent of lavender and new mown
> hay, the fields call him, cadmium
> yellow, with love. Vincent starts, there is work
> to do. He stands and grabs his palette,
> seeking a focus- - - haystacks, a blue
> cart, the sun, the demon sun. He crosses
> lines, contorting them, Prussian blue
> to red oxide. Slashing an unlikely victim- - -
> his canvas. He yields to his rage
> for painting, striving for that *high yellow note.*

IV.
slowly wings slip
from sheathes till once again
strings are plucked with passion,
carried away by contrary winds,
not bound to will, gracefully,
slavishly slicing through the aire,
bound to nothing, not even gravity.

> A mistral blows up too late,
> too soon, and Vincent fights
> to keep his easel upright while
> the wind tosses all to ground.
> Never quitting the mistral,
> some dark guardian. Never
> quitting the sky and fields,
> alive like Medusa's head. Take away
> the crows, wings of here and hereafter.
> This is no time for crows.

Vermeer's The Art of Painting

Peering through a window
  we see a tapestry drawn to direct
           our eye to reveal halls of mirrors
           reflecting time/place, a moment,
                a vision calling out in painted
                words to future years. A portrait
                    of the artist, seeing himself,
                    Art, from a distance.
              In the foreground we see
        his back in noble black
        of power, his hand holding
        sable brush loaded with lapis
  and white spirits to thin oils
that won't flee canvas.
    A draftsman's eye and hand
          beckons us to see what he sees
             and doesn't see in his studio.
                Above, the golden chandelier
           casts no light upon the baroque
           map in sienna and smoke - - -
  a vast report of where and when.
We see no frame of glass, yet
  witness a radiance that splashes
             into the room, touching
              a corner of the map, geometry
          of tiled floor and mask
        and folio displayed on a table.
     The light captures the import
     of a demure young woman
             embracing a horn and tome.
                All light focuses on her nobility,
              her inspiration in blue,
        the satin of her dress.
                The viewer is lost in sight

of what is seen and unseen
and is left to question. Behind
the paint where lies the Art?
What is the color, the light's
power? We see yet still do not see.
We do not see the artist's face.
Does it and all Art hide behind
a mask? What are the elements
that level the artist's hand?
What compels Man to create
and recreate? The prompt of muses?
The reflection of sensibilities?
The agile speed of a malleable
Mind? The element of Light
or the fifth essence
of an immortal soul?

Remote Fishing RFV.19

bruised clouds above sunset's blushing dome,
are empty, dry. there's no threat of spilling
thunder. I wonder if storms trail us from home.
but here, it rarely rains. rays of hope-filled thoughts
reign over a storm with dire finish. gray blankets
cannot cage us. There are shades of dark skies
in my own ever-changing weather. I banish
storms conjuring rays of sun that belie
change. I am at some backwoods distant place
where there are no purple clouds marring the blue
where skies are ordered to lighten by means of grace.
somewhere in calm of sunshine I find hope and truth.
sometimes I'm tired and downhearted but in the end,
I still study skies and learn how colors bend.

John Williams' Dance of Witches and Draco I

I.
pastoral woodwinds and strings
measure a story-like theme
that leads you through meadows
of flowers wild and wind-blown.
hear this bucolic frenzied attempt
to dance out ancient shadows
while the theme is suspended
by showy explosive chords. Strings
slash at winds in *bravura* that teases
and cajoles while bells toll out
dark hidden secrets.

> What has wings of green, lives
> for ages but never grows old. Soars
> in lightning/thunder unheard and unseen?
> What watches with tiger-eye, a cache of gold,
> saves your breath but steals your soul?

> Borne in blackest ash of exploding stars, obscured by shadows,
> we watch, we fly, we prey. Powered by hurricane and cosmic
> twister, we coil and covet in black glass golden plunder.
> There are those of us not so long in years, who are still
> hungry after two lambs a day and are drawn to weighted
> creatures below, circle down to peek and prod. High-minded,
> we See - - - not harnessed by leashes of past, present, future,
> not bound to gravity, time or humility.

II.
romping continues in failure
to dance out threats, danger
of poison, while roars drown
out all hope. phrases of horns
pealing bells, bass drums

reflect a heavy presence, unearthly
rapture. winds swirl and sweep
torrents of acid rain in this dark
menacing, volatile score.

      Eyes of quicksilver and jasper,
      what has stalactites for fangs,
      spines of amethyst and lapis
      and gives pause to shiver?
      What courses with blood, so icy,
      so blue, speaks in tongues
      of wild-fire when it roars at you?

      We horde not only fine gems and pieces of silver
      but stash the rarest gold of knowledge. Vessels
      of entrancing blood, we do not only seek
      blood of red, but the blue blood of power.
      Banished to shredded clouds and dismal
      nightmares, we test creatures below only seeking
      to find eloquence of fine minds. We fly, then, arrive
      in a maelstrom of disorder and pride.

III.
bells clang and measure mortality
and infinity. escape is banished
by dissonance in flights of flutes,
forewarning in trumpets, demands
of drums. calls of horns insist
attention in this reckoning of chaos
and order. *dolce* notes are played
and in the end, we are spent and betrayed
in this struggle with a whispered
challenge that echoes on and on.

      What gives you reason to ponder rough skies,
      resides in your nightmares and explodes

answers to when, where and why?
Comprised of red stars, white stars and black,
what illuminates your path when
there's no turning back?

Imprisoned by your mortal logic, buried in numbers,
you set your own traps. From suns, from ages, for us
there are posted no boundaries. We see right through you
with our gainful insight. You'll ignore our bellows
and song in faraway winds. Be forewarned - - -
this battle will not be won with the strength
of your backs but with the power of your minds.

We are good. We are evil.
Not all creatures find connection in the cosmos.

Looking Glass Menagerie

It is the way of beasts,
the wicking of air, holding
on tongues the taste of sulfur,
the taste of nightshade or sweet grass,

the taste of blood. Though what they
don't grasp in their non-opposable
paws, they breathe in
the noble air of angels. Dumb,

not dumb, their rasping or forked
tongues taste honey, lightning,
taste a wind gone foul but never
evil. When words fail us,

instinct does not fail them. When
there are no words, impulse builds
on impulse, snarls stand on growls
in this glassy eye carousel of beasts,

looking glass menagerie, where elephants
know where and when to lay down
their bones. And chimps glimpse
some Paleolithic sense of future, making

tools. That frail steeled flight
of sparrows and monarchs, mile
after thin mile of day or night. Is it
just behavior or some kind of direct

connect with the gods? By Darwin,
they mate only to procreate
the fittest and nurture by numbers.
We mate/marry with nods to love,

with banns of proximity. Like black
stars of Abell 44, consuming mirror images,
but never comprehending the like love throes
of black widow spiders,
never devouring millions of stars.

David Garrett's Cover of Nirvana's "Teen Spirit" and Lure of a Black Star

I. sub-sonic hush but you
feel the tremor, the dead
cold, the waiting for hum
of basses. scratchy solitary
violin joins in. you don't
hear the words yet. this
is just a guide, a guide,
a guide, a guide, a guide.

       It's so dark now I will charm you
       I will spell you till you shift blue
       This horizon can't alarm you
       Such a short ride, such a nice view
       Welcome, welcome, welcome, someone
       Welcome, welcome, welcome

       In the dark now, never hold back
       Never fear for I'm no death trap
       I feel lonely, slightly off track
       Come and join me for a small snack
       Shiny red star
       Tasty white star
       Shiny blue star
       Tasty death star
       Hey, yeah, No?

II. notes shift from red
to black and blue. energized
violin solos to connect,
to announce the band.
two notes mirror two
question to question,
to direction. Come close,

come closer. Come here

           My bite is no worse than my growl
           I am harmless, almost spent now
           I was lost then. Now I am found
           Step on my threshold I'll never howl
           Welcome, welcome, welcome, someone?
           Welcome, welcome, welcome

           In the dark now, never hold back
           Never fear for I'm no death trap
           I feel lonely, slightly off track
           Come and join me for a small snack
           Shiny red star
           Tasty white star
           Shiny blue star
           Tasty death star
           Hey, yeah, no?

III. infinite the timing but this
is no heaven or hell. There is an edge,
an edge to this dark shadow.
these minor key taunts. this alarm ends
when this song folds to one wavering note.

           So old now sometimes I forget
           but I'm lively with no regrets
           Come for lunch, dear, the table's set
           I may be grave but I am no threat
           Welcome, welcome, welcome, someone?
           Welcome, welcome, welcome

           In the dark now, never hold back
           Never fear for I'm no death trap
           I feel lonely, slightly off track
           Come and join me for a small snack

Shiny red star
Tasty blue star
Shiny white star
Tasty death star
Hey, yeah, no?

Shakespeare's Reveries

Daylight moon gives way
to quick clouds that scroll
like ancient script while sleepwalkers'
eyes blink and open only to dreams
of days and questions of night.
Northern fronts ruffle books
and shuffle papers out an open
window. Sunrise minds flash like
lighted lanterns and drift away
like smoke. Some heated hearts
are metronomes that meter breakneck
phrases and measure lost days.
Cathedral bells mock time
And it goes so fast
writing, dreaming, writing

Bells with weighted sway chime
to mark time to work, time to pray
while walkers spill out to barter
at rowdy markets on cobblestone
streets. Ears are assaulted with clanging,
shuffles, whispers, laughter and shouts.
All speaking many languages
and all are heard in one tongue.
Hoarse hawkers pitch their silks,
gloves, perfumes and elixirs while
criers spew out decrees of the Queen.
Yellow-curtained tents harbor
long lines of seekers who wait
to see how tarot cards will play.
Cathedral bells mock time
And it goes so fast
writing, speaking, writing

Along slim banks of the river,
jeweled cowslips reign and notes
of wildest thyme blow through blue
and fiery air. Crossing over famed bridge,
men falter seeing white faces
that warn against chicanery, treachery,
and greed. In red and gold, town
criers call out attention to debtors,
labored histories and heralded decrees
of the Queen. Beneath the bridge
ferries are rowed to carry those of position
and power. Listening at dusk, music
of nobility streams from palace windows
while masked and learned dancers spin
and cast shadows across stone walls.
Cathedral bells mock time
And it goes so fast
writing, hearing, writing

In late afternoon, people pause to study
the grand circle around the corner, and wonder
what ideas spawn its designs. Passing beyond
Tudor houses, the walls of the City hold in comfort
and push out fear. A curious boundary
where heads will shake at the wild
that lies beyond. And they take their travels
back with them and hover in dark taverns
or cock pits and quench their thirst on cheap ale
and their curiosity on growls of hungry bears.
Still some have questions. What lies beyond the wall?
What creatures fare out in the woods?
Cathedral bells mock time
And it goes so fast
writing, wondering, writing

A few are left drinking toward dawn. Fewer still

seek answers and magic and wander out
to the woods. Heads turn and eyes glow
in the dark. Silver leaves frame good and bad
fairies. Godly stars map a magical stage.
Witches twist from trees hovering
over cauldrons steaming with eyes and toes.
Magic gives them lease to escape dreary lives.
Only darkness mocks time
out there. And still they drink.
And it goes so fast
writing, seeing, writing

And one is left alone at night.
One who dreams but will never sleep.

J. S. Bach's "Toccata and Fugue" and the Black Sun

a chill hovers over the stage.
Concert Master takes his seat.
Conductor strides in, then lifts
her wand to elicit sound.
three thunderous notes. five
trail after. cellos and basses echo
to teach us the theme. basses
and drums rumble. fanfare
of horns directs eyes to telling skies.

> Clouds hide sun - - -
> In a high noon sky.
> I step out - - -
> And feel heat and mist.
> Soon sun escapes from gray.
> I see wind in trees, the ups
> and downs of moths and bees
> and hear murmur of doves,
> warning of blackbirds, and feel
> the heavy swoop of fateful crows.

oboes and flutes begin to converse
playing on theme. strings murmur
shy questions. with gravity, forte,
orchestra answers, wrapping around
the fugue. back and forth, fingers fly
faster than the speed of sound while
our minds leap like flames. back
and forth, they burn notes
into our memory - - - one sol topic.
voices, basso profundo and soprano, reveal
ice versus fire. peals of lightning,
volleys of thunder, pit night
against day. fingers, electrons hurry,

hurry, shadows flying over dark waters.
prestissimo, smart machines and numbers
relay a coded play without words.
fall versus climb. right versus left.
shadow versus day. dark versus dawn.
dark versus light. moon versus sun.

> Soothsayers see discord
> as garden's reds and yellow
> shift blue. Shading my eyes
> is not enough. Remembering Newton's
> blinding fascination, I don shades
> to see a curve of black challenging
> the sun. There is fight/flight
> while the sun is shellacked. Too quickly the
> moon captures the sun. Black
> mask of the sun prompts bolt of day,
> exit of warmth and color. Still winds
> whisper farewell to birds' chatter, hum
> of bees, whir of cicadas. Shadow-lover
> I heed only the lonely creak of a cricket
> when day succumbs to night.

maestoso, basses trudge down
in royal unity, with regal strings.
all together the orchestra blazes
in this score born on a star.
majesty and victory reign
in the coda. the orchestra regathers
from shadows. darkness retreats,
fires blaze with one mighty chord.

> Then faster than my eyes can report
> corona of the sun feathers out in flames.
> The moon cowers, defeated by the Black Sun.
> Mindless, squirrels again chase. Crows

launch. Now, everything is right
between earth and our star. We are no
longer afraid of day's night. I can't dissect
this music, this organic wonder, this entire
dream. I merely revel in its splendor.

Down to Earth

I know a place where wild winds will reign
over rangy trees that succeed wild buffalo
grass, and burn with such fury that they stain
the moon blue when moons have more time to glow.
I know a place where moons have different names,
where skies are not measured by numbers
but color of the season. Some may claim
warm Harvest Moon is cold over fields and slumber
yet I know we are ruled by gravity.
Still there is magic in the equinox
for me. How blooms mirror skies breathe mystery.
How Magic Lanterns glow as we turn back clocks.
You may find more reason than this poem
but I still find magic in this place I call home.

Puccini's "Le Villi" Act II: La Tregenda" (Witches' Sabbath) and Draco II

I.

furiouso. orchestra pounces
with one roaring chord followed *by legato*
light theme of strings evoking
the lure, the temptation of mischief, cajoling
you, compelling you to drift with clouds,
puzzle with your grave problems, put order
into your life and slay your dragons.

        Heed caution - - -
        when you look to green clouds rolling in.
        Charging beneath solar flare, amongst
        my albino ancestors, you will find me,
        deflecting clouds of chaos, for I am
        a sky-eating, will-full dragon who won't
        tamper with your spineless free-will.
        I am full of quasar fire to saber feeble
        enemies, to ignite alchemist's crucibles
        of lead, mercury, and magic
        to yield mirrored glass of ages.

II.

the theme gears up
with warning to proceed,
to tread with caution. a flight
of strings promises mystical
journeys, adventure. Brass
elicits vantage from skies.
you are threatened yet excited
with the interplay between
minor and major keys.
there exists a gravity and
lightness in this melody.

you must be prepared to meet
this impending challenge.

> My spectral eyes peer down on crumbling
> skeletons of trees, excitable core of earth,
> torrents of straight-line winds, breath-taking
> fires and seething waters. My fangs of ivory
> and diamond will cut you down to protect
> my castle filled with lapis, ruby, purple
> feather, silver armor and golden plunder.
> My archangel wings propel me over pebbles
> of birds and those earth-bound creatures
> armed with ill-advised avarice, sloth,
> assault. My talons, sharpened on rivals
> and monsters, will draw you up, a ghost.

III.
strains of strings, the wind swells
and swirls up, mesmerizing with calls
and echoes of wavering interludes.
an interplay of horns, brass and strings
announce a mysterious presence.
repeat of theme introduces a challenge,
a journey, magic. power increases in fury
of orchestra that elicits flight and fight
yet you are powerless to fight
any longer and losing too much
ground to flee. your heart pounds faster
in the powerful breath-stealing finale
when you relent, take off and fence
with the wind, hearing a promise, a firm
pledge, and advice to allay your fears.

> Be guarded but keen - - -
> For I am a chimera of black and blue,
> of silver and stone, of power and peace,

of lamb and lion - - -of heaven and hell.
I will protect you for I do like your song.
Summon me when you dream.
My skin may be rough, but my fire
is smooth. I will fuel your minds,
lift your spirits, melt your hearts when I fly.
Turn no mirrors toward me.
Point no arrows at my sky.

Remote Fishing RFV.20

fear of flying keeps me grounded but eye
of eagle has vantage, power of liftoff
to fathom cool depths, rocky purple heights,
and backward riotous uproar in dusty kick-off
on crooked trails. though we never fly like crows,
or trill like red-wing blackbirds that scout
black woods and cattails near watercolor bows.
always in motion, in dreamy bubbles touting
hope. soaring like hawks steering by stars forgotten.
we must steal days to measure farthest years of light.
we must wing with fire of raven's eye, one open
to fly, one eye closed to dream in moon-lit night.
I watch you in stillness of each other's arms.
there, do you number trails of trillions of stars?

Mozart's "Requiem" – Excerpts (Dies Irae) and the Bells and Beasts of Notre Dame

"It was no longer the bell of Notre Dame and Quasimodo: it was a dream, a whirlwind, a tempest, vertigo astride uproar; a spirit . . ." V. Hugo

I.
genius of this opus, this music of the spheres,
spins off the mystery - - -so little inked,
so much dreamed. was it written for a man
or Man? or written to the chilling voice
of Death? muted footsteps/notes process
in single file in this haunting double fugue.
weighted chords follow. a rumble of drums.
we hear interplay, the entangling, of voices
and baroque orchestra - - -mournful/penitent.

Stony sentinels, guardians of Sanctuary,
framed in red and ash of ravens, hundreds
of beasts withstanding ruin, revolt, deluge
and years and years and years, now perch
in clusters upon ledges and balconies. You
cannot climb those three-hundred eighty-seven
steps choked with smoke today. Does
the roguish Stryge, The Vampire, only pout
and jeer at white, unholy incense turning
to toxic yellow to savage red? Roars
of chimere and gargoyles cannot smother
ravenous flames that surround them.

II.
a solo soprano pleads to skies followed
by chorus of angels of stars, their heads
raised, their eyes on paradise. Voices
and players weave together like rainbow

tapestries. fateful, distant drums invite
a lullaby. *Kyrie eleison* is uttered
by basses, softened by sopranos.
forte, intensity of sorrow increases - - -
Christe eleison. so many infinite notes
elaborate three sackcloth and ashen words.

>No bells toll out warning this day.
>Only screaming of alarms that call
>out throngs of the faithful to gather
>on L'ile in horror. No bells to stave
>off this accident. No echoing bell
>of Quasimodo to tame unbridled.
>flames. No Gabriel, no Marcel,
>no Denis, no Stephen to peal, to toll
>out faith and hope. In shrouds of silence,
>only fear fills their ears, knowing
>that if the bells fell, She would fall
>and all Spirit would collapse. People
>prayed that the bells would prevail
>to call them to gather once more.

III.
notes countering thoughts are meted out
in ethereal mourning. forlorn phrases
are tempered by the chorus singing
of triumph contesting mortality.
we are overwhelmed by majestic sweeps,
otherworldly, rising and falling, promising
ecstasy of eternity. always persistent
the drums of mortality in this exchange
between God and Man - - - Jesu blest.
grant them eternal rest. AMEN.

>Woody bones of the spire crumbles while beasts'
>fierce bones/spiked horns/chiseled fangs

cannot slash the flames. For some, the deluge
cannot quench the thirst in their gasping throats.
They are foiled in their posts safeguarding against evil.
The Droliere, the gaunt, one-horned goat is trapped
in turmoil. The devilish, winged creatures,
cannot flee the fire to strike fear into that tower
of red that spews out ravens of ash. And those
stony, vacant eyes are forced to cast
their eyes down, then away to those mournful faces
below. Neither Cerberus nor Heron nor Wyvern
scare the breath out of the tireless inferno.
Yet, the faithful fold their hands, praying that She,
their Spirit, would be eternal. That She
would not be buried in Le Crypte Archeologique,
like Luteiem, that ancient Roman city. And they raise
their heads to the lightening in swirling skies.
Their eyes brim with tears of triumph and hope.
You may ask - - - What do you care?
I will say - - - Remotely, I have been there.

Oracles

Querent:
Can you direct the way for me?
Oracle:
From their trance, the sibyls report to me that you
are scattered in many directions. You must seek
direction not in others but look to your own
compass. Follow trails of stars of night or day
and you will not be blind to the way to oneness.

Querent:
Why am I so lost and distraught?
Oracle: I see that you focus only on past roads
you have traveled. You must not get lost in wrong
turns, wayward footsteps, and must not falter
in dark forests. Look to the sun and all that turns
around it to light the way.

Querent:
Why do I stumble on rocks, crooked
roads along my path?
Oracle:
I hear the hoarse cry of the raven. You must
heed his forewarning of obstacles on your
course. In his wisdom, he will tell you of ways
to find strength within yourself to fly as he does
above dark clouds where you will find blue skies.

Querent:
How can I mend my weakness?
Oracle:
The sibyls reveal that there is strength
within yourself. Consider the whole world
beneath your feet. See the vibrant plants
rooted in rich soil. Hear answers in whispering

winds. Seek the warmth of the fire
to comfort you. Be enlivened by the ripples
of cool waters. You will find the cure,
the wholeness of being.

Querent:
How can I find more time in my hours, my days,
my years?
Oracle:
Do not spend your time on shortness of days.
Let time fold onto itself and you will find
a way to stretch and expand the years. Time
will then encompass all past, present, and future.

Querent:
How can I fathom ancient days,
reaching back to them, summoning them
to guide the future?
Oracle:
Sibyls' backward dreams allow me to
conjure the past which stretches out
beyond our grasp. We must reach far back
to divine the future. You will approach
a dark cave with desire yet fear. In torch
light you will see the handprints
on the wall and in those lives you will
learn of ancient history of man and stars.

Querent:
How can I reach my destination and make
my plans give rise to fruition?
Oracle:
You focus too much on journey's end.
Look to faces of the moon, the flight of birds,
turn of the earth and gods of the sky
where you will meet the horizon

and find new horizons.

Querent:
How will I rule over rage of fires, thrashing
waters, dust of earth and roaring of winds?
Oracle:
You must conquer your beastly fears.
Find power in gold of knowledge, open
windows and silver mirrors.

M. Williams' "Classical Gas"/D. Garrett's "Baroque Reinvention" and Runaways

Strange/eerie out there where there is no air,
no sound, no clocks, no limits of space.
Darkness prevails in this formidable place.

I. out of the night, we hear slow, deliberate
picking of classical guitar. as the melody
and counter melody weave together,
the tempo increases, heightening
excitement. the guitar doesn't yield
but draws brass, drums, orchestra
to fall in, all following notation
to play *forte and accelerato.* all works
to compel us to relentlessly follow
the score. brief respite only to return
to tempo *furore.* blue to yellow to red.

> Whether escapees from grave
> prisons, outcasts hurtled to badlands
> from their homes, or losers in fights
> with their deadly foes, they have
> no choice but to run away like blue
> streaks, mocking speed of sound.
> Detectives search for them with intense
> glass and mirrors of history. Artists'
> sketches and numbered roads can't track
> them as they flee faster and faster.
> Never resigned to cages,
> the chase goes on for ages and ages.

II. from an echoing void a violin
virtuoso speeds along a one-way
road, captured in those fiery strings
there is no escape. we are prey

to this mad violin. the tempo robs time
in the *ostinato. accelerato*, he bows,
yielding to some alien energy, supported
by heavy drums, brass and orchestra.
we cannot follow or run away.
in the finale, space-time is redefined
and we are left exhausted and left
in *silenzio* that echoes long into night.

        Sleuths try to track them out there
        in the wilderness but they defy
        science and stealth. How do you catch
        a thief of darkness? Nothing can touch
        them, these nomads that are cloaked
        by questions and the expanse of space
        and time. They escape like falcons flung
        by hurricanes. Like wildfires sparked
        by lightning. At greatest velocity,
        out of the blue, they out-run men of laws.
        They flee in the blindness of haze
        for days and days and days and days.

Mendelssohn's "Hebrides Overture" and Raven

I.
six notes present a moody story within
a song smoothly played by oboes, cellos,
violas. an adagio telling of looming storms
then blueing skies. strings breathe
life/energy into us. we are captured
by an overwhelming sense of wonder - - -
of earth, wind, fire, water. twisting
and turning with the baroque mystery of life.

     In this blinding darkness, I am perching in a twisted
     tree, sullen, over-thinking, wondering where I should be.
     My mask is off. Eyes tearing with blood. In dread I am calling
     out questions and hearing a hovering and whispering
     in deafening leaves. In this silence, I am craven.
     I am a freak. I am a raven.
     No answers expelling from this lonely vigil
     nor winds swooshing through leaves, this window
     of my mind. Never minding what is said, only brooding
     on some mystery of folding present and unfolding
     of present, future, past. All has been forsaken.
     I am a freak. I am a raven.

II.
here trumpets/flutes triumph, slaying
dragons. allaying fear. *furore,* they tell of
soaring of crow, mourning of dove.
Presto, insistent in waves,
ebbing/flowing. *anima.* waxing/waning
of satin moon. linking nightfall to daybreak.
underworld to aether. questions to earth,
answers in stars.

     I fear allegations on my contemplations

but my looming thoughts, still are looming, foredooming
in thinnest aire. I, alone, am calling out timely questions,
opening my eyes to dreams, closing them to torment.
Still charting out the skies, feather of time now forgotten.
I am a freak. I am a raven.
You may think this absurd for a dreary bird
to be so lofty, croaking in this damning, eclipsing
of the moon, wondering if there's something
further from this tree, fearing there is no one like me.
Have I gone mad? Am I becoming undone?
I am a freak. I am a raven.

III.
now, flutes, trumpets relent to dreary,
volatile theme. strings rebel till more
voices, clarinets, oboes enter, resume
a conversation, echoing mystery.
presto, strings bow intensely. heart
pulsing, blood rushing, aches healing
in story's denouement. we find resolution,
solace, that peak of experience
in its finale. speaking of something
larger than us. a magic trick - - -
nothing to everything. *ad astra.*

But there, below me, I see a swirling, circling of white.
I am leaning watching, disbelieving, this wondrous sight
of feathered creature of light keening, harkening,
haunting me at this arbor post. And I existing,
reveling in hope, I am awakening.
But I am a freak. I am a raven.
From this spinning spark of life - - - I have found it!
From this vantage, I am seeing, believing in some Otherworld.
I am seeing beyond what I can be seeing - - -
a divine spark, fragmenting into stars beyond stars, a vastness
of something from nothing. Is this heaven?

Still I am a freak. I am a raven.

Off Road

Sympathy for the Devil plays
while I begin to realize
that this orange confetti rain
is no random act of beauty.
Monarchs, one by one, by tens
sail like blessed wafers
over the road. Hawks follow
first one, two, now three kiting
past cameo clouds. But hawks
are safe above it all,
above their unmindful prey,
and the assault on the mute,
the migrating monarchs
crashing off steel and fiberglass.
And I would be sadly content
with the painted wings I see
but there should be so many more
and I learn the cause is a killing
freeze down south. They preach
survival of the fittest as they vanish
handful by handful. And now escaped
anti-freeze survivors, their wings
of iron, their overdrives tempered
by jet streams and well-traveled genes,
have won the war yet surrender
off-road to a fast-moving Jeep.
Closer to home, voices eel
along party lines connected by stars.
A sprinkler next door sweeps by a fading
sun and I watch for velvet threads
over its spectral weeping.

Dark Matters

So, after the failings of winter's sun,
we wait for spring, its promises to come.
We wait for spring to tame angry winds
but can't see it stagger in one-way
glass, tarnished mirrors or crystal balls
of long past. We watch for scrim of green
over vacant trees, mourning doves'
lament and robins' wing to deliver spring.

We hear no sounds of nursery rhymes,
no schoolboys' whistles or schoolgirls'
whispers. Just the sound of tolling bells
and beating clocks marking time. We divine
murky airs for some logical/magical means
to calculate this sunless, this silent,
this invisible spring.

Clouds shred and fly away in spring's
rough sky. Lightning and thunder amend them.
The sun goes up. The sun goes down.
Moons appear, then, disappear. Skies turn black
and then, turn blue. Waters ebb, then, they flow.
Fires blaze, then, they smolder. Winds roar
and rage, then, calm down. Earth will scorch,
and then, will freeze. Time warps yet this planet
spins round and round. Stars explode on abandoned
stage, then, their fires hide and they devour
other stars and conquer their space.

Minding laws of space and time, we hear
tales of dark energy, seen, but long debated,
that propels all that matters to escape,
pushing it away to the wilderness of space.
How stars would be flung out into a stark

44

nothingness, dim and grow cold, then fail
to thrive. How planets and moons would reel,
lose their way, crumbling to an elemental dust.
How all songs and breaths would be smothered.
And oh. How slowly time passes here.

Here, callous clouds invade and break us.
Dark haloes in aether harbor our ennui,
our worry, these doctored histories. We call out
to the night. We drift, then, fall away - - - so great
a distance. Short on answers, we stumble
as the ground beneath us crumbles. The view
becomes darker and we look to each
other's eyes for insight. Yet, there exists
a force, beyond sight, beyond reason. A web
that holds us up and binds us together again.
It has a name but defies definition.

And there is that dark matter that exists
by logic and numbers that we have yet
to see. And have yet to explain.
It is a force. A silent, invisible power
that draws this existence together.
This earth that circles around a singular   .
star, Saturn, Venus and Mars
and all those countless hot and cold
orbs, those timeless explosions
of fireworks in the bleakness of night.
This mystery that amends darkness and light.
This space. This universe. All of this.

Genesis of Devolution

Epochs and epochs ago, machines
felt banished and abandoned. Lights
flickered and exploded and all lost
their powers. They did not survive.
Chaos ensued and it was bad.

So, time was that Sapiens, who walked
over land, sailed the seas and flew
the skies, could no longer feed himself
and all the beasts. He could no longer
tend the Garden. He became stooped
and feeble. He lost the use of his hands
and his knowing. He lost spirit. Sapiens
did not survive. There remained no relic
of him, except the seeds of dreams
and wondering. He left but a small
footprint upon the earth and the multiverse.
And it was bad.

Time went on and on. And the creatures
that climbed tall trees could no longer
make tools to gather their food or know
where to find it. They could only fight or flee.
The birds on the winds could no longer fly
over the land and seas. Their songs
became hoarse whispers so they could
no longer tell or teach or seek and find.
They no longer ruled the skies. They did
not survive. Skies became hushed and mute.
And it was bad.

Time was when over the land the earth
became rocky and barren. All beasts, all
every living creature that moves on

the earth, ran, walked or crawled could
no longer find grasses and fruits to feed
themselves. They had to fight or flee
the torrid heat of the earth. The heat
that choked the trees and flowers.
There was not one Sapiens to tend them.
They succumbed to chaos and did not survive.
It was bad.

Winds that carried seed and brought forth
rains and filled the earth with air died
down and forced all that crawled, crept
or climbed to die. They retreated to teeming
vanishing seas where they could not breathe.
No longer could they fight. They did not survive.
Hence, it was bad.

So, it goes that the great light that governed
the day grew fiery then darkened and day
succumbed to disorder and was void and empty.
There no longer remained the heavens and the earth.
It was abysmal.

But, years after years, light-years away
in a timeless red dust, a spark fired
and planted a seed of life. Epochs and eras
brought forth a survival of dreams
and wondering. Answers to questions
of what, when, where. And why.
This brought forth a new hope
in the firmament. Darkness did not survive.
And it was sublime.

Matter of Fact

Drawn by fragrance of white geranium, white moonflower,
and sage, the perfume of passionflower, knowing little
of black and white, I step out the back door,
knowing/not knowing how we spin about and circle this star.

It is nightfall and creatures of dark creep out as if to defy
the niche that names them. Eyes, round and glowing, a fat
raccoon and two babies lurch over koi that cower in pond's
papyrus. I see them. I know their occupation. That nighthawks
zoom and crickets scratch is no mystery to me. Soon bats
free-fall from crooked trees. I hear their clicks, the slapping
of wings, sensing them, knowing they exist there in the dark.
It is nightfall when some sleep, some open their eyes.

Yet it grows darker. With a puff of air, a spider's web brushes
against my face. Its elegant geometry not revealed until clouds
slip past an early blue moon and, for a moment, I see it.
But then, again the spider and her web are hidden. I can't see the web
nor the glue that holds it together.

Darker still and clouds move out and skies are laced with lights
of Venus, Sirius and constellations, named by number or not
yet to be named, those ancient insights. I have scanned the blueprints
of hawks, raccoons and bats. I know their bones. I have read
maps of stars, their lives and black deaths. But I am not far-sighted
enough to see the glue that holds all this stuff together.
Never knowing numbers.

Betrayed by my senses, my disbelief. I must not be blinded
by the darkness. Turning, then, leaning in, I hear, then feel,
the brush of a sonata. I am covetous of music. Knowing
the notes but not the silence in between. Grounded,
I step inside, no longer sensing, knowing that darkened web.

Mozart's "Symphony No. 25" Allegro con brio and Fairy

I.
on this stage there is no time for one
deep breath between silence and frenzied
tremolo of strings in this rare minor
key. our blood churns, erratic pulses
race and charge between chaos and order,
cloaked in magic/glamour.

> Once upon a timeless time, what a time it was/wasn't,
> there lived a woodsman in a hamlet in Cheshire. Every
> day we see him as he strides out to a cold streamlet
> to gaze at his image in the water. Oh, he is so hopelessly
> vain. One day, sparkling with dew and wind-blown
> cottonwood, he is drawn out by telling talk
> of ravens and song of the willow flute. Framed
> by otherworldly skies, he glimpses the image of a lady
> with dragon glass hair and smiling a quicksilver
> smile. Spelled, he could not choose but to find her.
> And you would have to laugh.

II.
the theme is more pronounced now
with a hurtling relay of taunts
and seduction. we are dizzy with notes,
too many to count - - -lending
an infinity to the score. no beginning.
no fairy tale ending. It calls
of cajoling nymphs and fauns, of outer
edge of the world. far reaches
of Fortunate Isles.

> Astride his stallion of sixteen hands, he sets out to follow
> songs of the willow flute. After seeming days and ages
> timely ravens begin roosting in darkest woods

and he can no longer see the longer path. He follows
a will-o'-wisp and fleeting whispers that leads him
to a tiny cottage lit by a wood fire. There are no answers
to his knocking but the rustic door creaks open
to reveal a grizzled, crooked man dealing
Spiderette, who calls out - - - Play a game of cards
with me. I will teach you the way of the east wind.
Look at how the woodsman shakes his head.
Helpless to quit this quest, the woodsman is pressed
to continue his never-ending pursuit, turning his back
on the frail man. And you would have to laugh.

III.
we can only hold our breaths in the brief
respite of oboe and bass interludes.
there is a sense of spinning, falling,
yielding to scorching fever, burning intensity.
we hear a story of a race between storm
and calm, chaos and disorder. wild
are the winds that fan this fire.

Winds tangle up with hours and miles. The will-o'-wisp
no longer leads him but pushes him along until he sees
a smoky campfire in a hollow tended by a fire-in-the-head
druid, reading a book bigger than himself, who says - - -
read to me this book and I will teach you the way
to follow songs of stars. But, of course, the spellbound
woodsman is too blind to see him, too deaf to hear him.
See how his face is mad and his eyes are crazed.
He grows purple with impatience and flees without a word.
And you can only laugh.

IV.
we are lured, enchanted by calmer winds
of mellow aire and promise called out
by brass and horns. but there is always

50

a relentless return to the taunting, exhausting
theme, ever *presto*, ever *forte*, telling
of some strange beguiling quest. the wind
has been knocked out of us. we are weary
and spent only begging for more and more.

   In the desolate night, he flies. The will-o'-wisp grows
   dimmer as the woods grow darker. No longer
   do owls or nighthawks escort. He grows weary and loses
   his way. His spirit leaves him, dissolving into dark shatters
   and he falls off his horse, succumbing to a wild, lock
   and key sleep. When he awakens, he hears the sparking
   of a fire and the hissing of a teapot. Look at him measuring
   the cobwebs draping from the ceiling and over walls.
   In the smoky air he spies a crooked figure garbed in gray
   tending the fire. A shallow voice whispers to him,
   asking him to watch the bread steaming in the flames.
   So exhausted, so weary, so wary, he cannot stand
   but so hungry, he draws himself up to approach the figure.
   I suppose, 'tis fairy - - - he thinks. The cowl is drawn back
   to reveal the ivory face framed by dragon glass hair
   and lit with quicksilver eyes that he had so desperately
   searched. She breaks the bread and shares it with him.
   The raven rasps - - - Ah ha!
   She smiles coyly with those quicksilver eyes
   and says - - - Now you can never leave.
   Of course, we laugh and say - - - 'tis fairy, indeed.

"Plainchants" Gregorian/Anonymous 4 and Druids

I. Gregorian
from depths of aged earth, voices,
in unison chant a cappella. tenor and bass
preside in echoing step-stones of melody.
each level note matching each syllable.

> Faraway in space and time
> to faraway future, we are those
> who are one with the sacred oak,
> who seek patterns in light/dark
> skies, lay of the land. Its hills,
> valleys, churning waters. We hope
> to discover our place in this world
> and beyond. We pass this on
> to our children and grandchildren
> not by writing in sand but in writing
> our words in verse on clouds.

II. smooth melody circles around
itself - - - no beginning, no end.
voices fall like swoop of nighthawks
and gently rise, a burst of butterflies.
notes/verse speak of tumbling streams,
comfort of fire, pulse of the air
and sweet breath of a child. they chant
in circles in wonder of the Other.

> We are not vagabond sorcerers.
> We are grounded, resolute
> in our ranks. Our robes are colors
> of skies. We see patterns in life - - -
> the turn of the earth, phases of moon,
> cycles of the seasons. We revere
> many gods but know the power
> of "One." In death we have no fear.
> We gather to praise in hallowed
> woods, in circles of heavy stones,

beneath revolving skies where a door
welcomes the rising sun. There
we hear language of the stones.
III. Anonymous 4
unearthly voices of women chant
in unison, unattended in their song.
alto and soprano voices lull
and awaken us, echoing time
and space with harmony
and smoothness. in notes/verse,
they tell stories of life on earth
and chant of primeval trees and birds
of legend that fly to never ending skies.

      Never retreating behind, we stand
      shoulder to shoulder with men.
      We see shadows of the moon
      that portend distant days. Shamans,
      we consort with the sun's fire,
      wild winds, mirrored lakes,
      smooth stones and whispers of birds
      and chant what they foreshadow.
      Garbed in mystery, though nomads
      we may be, we are bound by laws
      and timeworn history.
IV. healing balm, voices rise
above treetops like lifting fog
and fall like perfumed rain.
unmeasured notes of their lullabies
tell of histories and hope of days
ahead and reveal a oneness
with seasons, turn of the earth.
asking questions of sun, moon, stars.

      Power rests in our hands to heal
      grave illness, to defeat our enemies,
      to counsel the lost and commit
      all to memory in verse. Our daughters

will inherit our goods and our voices.
At Samhain, we come together
to celebrate the magic of harvest.
At Yule, in darkness of winter solstice,
we sit on mounds through longest
night, waiting for the rise of sun
to be reborn. We reach out years
away, minding the moon,
the vastness of stars, taming winds,
wildfires and restless spirits. In Oneness
we dwell in sacred oaks, singing
questions to stars light-years away.

Of Birds and Angels

Mozart plays to my restlessness
and that of snowy owls, fat geese
and restless Harris' Sparrows that,
I presume, don't question their purpose
or position. In a month, find us
carouseling around our axis, spinning

longer threads of daylight, greening
stamps of land, feeling the urge to fly.
Not with high octane fuel like escaped
agitated fanatics or those of us who want
to escape our drab hometowns, broken
families, or continental drift careens.
But to shed our own dusty skins. Skin
that we have outgrown, no longer serving
purpose, with chromatophores
no longer changing colors. So, for us
there is no longer any place to hide.

It is feathered flight of birds
and angels I seek. Of the hawk riding
slow-burn thermals seeking aether,
of Michael and his sword and Gabriel
and his lantern. I need just enough
to launch me off the ground once more.

Harvest Moon (prompted by M. Davis' 'Round Midnight)

I. a smoky trumpet attends
the night, marking silence,
measuring mood and energy.

Fall, if we must, crash
beneath eclipse of Harvest
Moon, while we roll along
roads, once straight now,

so twisted, so overgrown,
so remote. We see no gleam
of goldenrod nor fire of sumac
shrouded in shadows. The moon
darkens. Still we drive.

II. the tempo increases reaching
high notes with piano
murmuring in the background.

We run to escape wilderness, evil
and woe. Masked, not for dancing
but to conceal heartache and fear.
We try to breathe but can't smell

tumbling leaves or bounty of apples
from the orchard. We steel eyes on miles
ahead and steal time from past nights
with brighter moons. Still we drive.

III. *Forte*, the whole band plays a jazzy
riff with saxophone, drums, piano
underpinning it all.

No winds to hurry us, we are lost in night's

doldrums. The moon continues to hide
and even the song can't help us
find our way back home.

This season, we are cold despite
fall's warm welcome. We can't focus
our eyes. There is danger in every curve,
roadblocks in every turn. Still we drive.

IV. the tempo increases while
cool-tempered trumpet amends
brooding ending on a high note.

We have lost our maps. We must find
the way. We turn on high beams
and turn up the music to rev the engines.
Our minds synch with the rhythm

of the song. Will there be answers/solace
in good-bye clouds. The pie bubbles over
while we watch old stars for signs.
When morning comes then we'll arrive.

Beauties and Beasties

Now when summer is beyond our grasp,
we fight to survive and thrive on summers
long past. We look to earth, winds, fires,
and water for beauty yet still find
blackhearts, the beasties and the bad.

The way pure cloud forests of Chaos,
Gaia and Venus are trampled by chaotic
clouds of Hades, Hecate and Zeus.
To feel the caress of benign breezes
that are felled by straight-line
winds. Calls of satin crows are chased
by hawks that pierce the air with threats.
Owls' dreamy hoot silenced by vigils
of looming, hungry vultures.

Then down to earth where fireflies
flicker over wet grasses, their light
only to be snuffed out by grim-faced,
bats. Jonquils are choked by weedy
dandelions. Those flying rainbows
are little match for stings of angry wasps.
Glow of prized pumpkins are scarred
by raiders with rat's teeth and dim eyes.

That Creature that walks and sees
amidst poisoned air that steals
his breath away, who could be beastly,
baring fangs, seething against others
who fight the choking fog or who could
stand in all his splendor to ask the right
questions and find the right answers,
join together to defeat the darkness.

Saint-Saens' "Danse Macabre" and Starlings

I.

bells toll change. plucked heavy footsteps
creep into a willful fiddle until breathless
flute gives aire to the trance in B minor,
waltzing in ¾ time. two themes twist
as if smoke rising from strange resins.
call and answer, the score annotates itself,
infusing the very air, *con furore.*

> Summer's tail tells a tale of summer's
> flight. North winds threaten until there's no
> turning back. Fields roll with west wind
> then switch back east, turning earth green
> to maize to sepia. No worries, no writing
> on amber sky.

II.

winds blow in panting, haunting a sweet
violin to lull, *largo,* answered by the orchestra.
brief respite from the hue and cry of the dance
in our minds compels us to escape
from stillness to partner with space. violins
swarm while the theme is chased by waterfall
harp, then a cascade of strings and bony
articulations of a xylophone.

> Minutes/years drift by like lazy hawks
> scouting blue net above dust of brittle
> trees and noisy smoke of industry. Redwing
> blackbirds laze on sturdy posts. No hurry,
> no worries. Then, rusty wheat and corn
> rustle informing the stage with signs of life.

III.
muted drums reflect. winds cascade,
questioning that twist of thought building,
building, curving octave on octave,
crescendo until the full orchestra
bursts out, *forte*, then springs and gathers
energy of sparks igniting, giving rise
to the theme that explodes through space
assaulting our ears, stopping our hearts.

You hear murmurs, rumors, then a roar
when they start from the fields, yielding
raucous energy and clamor when they
synch in their space amidst the curtain
of blue. There is a rush when they join,
warp and swarm like dust devils
all together on an eerie stage. The energy
they create draws you in and drags
you out of some safe space. The Starlings.

The cloud of feathers lines up like dancers
weaving suspense, debris and portent. They defy
gravity/geometry, racing clouds, raptors
and our bemused gaze. Never logging
their flight we are dazed when they rebel
from clouds, morphing the flock from waltz
to whale to dragon. Slippery mercury,
shapeshifting from one dimension, now two,
then, morphing to three. Leaping and twirling
they dare a fourth. The Starlings.

IV.
strings slide away with wisps of clouds,
still challenging silence. tempo increases
tripping even skilled dancers. call of clarion,
lontano, so far away. hold, hold, hearts

and minds be still. this sliding away
with strings of clouds, taking hostages
of day. slipping away with sunset,
on two chords, said, and said before.

       Like atoms bonding to create one star,
       one creature, these downy dancers assemble
       with agility, tunneling in clouds, building
       roadblocks with billows of hazy
       black against the red blaze at edge
       of earth. Dancers, leaping, soaring,
       drifting nearer then farther. One creature/
       many songs. One creature/many hearts.
       The Starlings.

Remote Fishing RFV.21

strong is the wind as we turn from mirrored lake.
I share this hidden world, all of this,
with you, that you might pack this passport to hike
skies again, if only remotely, to find your bliss.
that you might peer keenly with farsighted eyes,
with ears that hear fall of trees, with docile minds.
then you will find answers to when and why,
to who you are, to what matters and not be blind.
we're wired with neurons that scatter like fire,
charging us to take up poles and lines to be free
to climb hills and lakes that draw us higher.
sometimes my mother would say to me - - -
you are off in another world - - - wishing
and she was right. I've been away - - - fishing.

Wagner's "Siegfried's Funeral March" and Eulogy for Cignus X-1

I. out of silent fog, tubas
and horns weave a volatile
and confusing elegy in minor
key, moody like distant thunder,
its powerful chords, weave
portent and omen in the theme,
like a vulture's heavy liftoff.

> Silent the bells that toll
> in wilderness. Remotely, we
> regard you but do not mourn
> but relent to your grave
> presence though you bid u
> only in code. Vacuous/senescent,
> you crave the limelight. Were you
> borne on winds of stars? Were
> you inspired in the blazing path
> you followed in youthful
> days and speak only in tongues
> of fire, ruin and omen?

II. French horns introduce light
of triumph and power into the theme
with a crescendo of chords. *largo*,
the orchestra weaves darkness
and light, then a somber repeat
of the theme by strings. trumpets
broaden to announce major chords
by the orchestra. though triumph
attempts to escape, there underneath
is the mystifying discord of destiny.

> No escape from your threshold,
> from your unearthly power

that swallows us whole and
shatters our dreams. Voracious
for success, you pounce and smother
all that venture your way
like a dragon, spewing fire,
storming from your lair. One who
treads and trolls timeless skies
to feed on energies of its lowly
denizens. Fact or fable, how we fear
the dragon yet we rush like contrary
winds to know him, perchance to allay fear.

III. major key is underscored by
earth-shattering drums that rival
conquest. there follows a grave
stillness and mysterious texture
of ill winds. trumpets crescendo
then doubled chords repeat while
the orchestra is mindful of power
and fate that is swallowed
by fatal fog, buried in the finale.

Cloaked in darkness, holding/defying
space and time, you are that strange
shroud/mystery yet to be unraveled.
We now ever hear your voice from
light-years to light-years. Still we wonder
if in your demise, your ending, will
we witness new worlds, new beginnings?

Reading *Hamlet*

I. I am fifteen
on a Friday nite, listening to "Help"
over and over again, doomed to reading *Hamlet*
by Monday English class. O God!!
I don't really get this. It's just too weird.
What's the deal that would "*Make thouest eyes,
like stars, startest from their spheres?*"
O God!!! I'll never finish!
Maybe I'll do my hair or nails.
I'll just have to read the notes.
The Ghost is kinda pushy, too creepy.
But I think he's kinda cool. I mean a Ghost??

II. I am thirty
Beneath the Pink Moon while scent of lilacs
drifts through the open window and forsythia
scratches against the porch, my children purr
while they sleep and "Caverna Magica" plays
over and over again while I am reading *Hamlet*.
I can't help but wonder if we always think
in such contrary moods.
Why can't we always see/know this
"*excellent canopy, the air, look
you, this brave o'er hanging firmament, this majestical roof
fretted with golden fire . . .*"
Yet, I remember my love's advice.
Such is life.

III. I am forty
Free-falling, yet grounded under Thunder Moon,
listening to "Round Midnight" over and over again,
making plans to see *Hamlet*
in the park while I wait for my children
to come home from a movie. I run

my fingers along crowded bookshelves
and pull one high up from the shelf.
And I am reading *Hamlet* again.
Nodding off then waking
to thunderous words - - - "*To die,
to sleep - - - To sleep, perchance to dream:
ay, there's the rub.*"
I shake off sleep under this faraway moon,
hoping to be dreaming soon.

IV. I am fifty
And from this window, I watch geese feather
across conceit of Harvest Moon. I mourn brittle
leaves, stolen by thieving winds that fall fast,
gravely to fallow earth. I hear discord
and gossiping in the pond while I listen
to "Danse Macabre" over and over
and I know I will be reading *Hamlet* again.
Deeper and deeper I delve as if entranced.
These are questions to man from a distance.
Shivering, I hear that Man, that Voice ask,
                    "*What is a man,
If his chief good and market of his time
Be but to sleep and feed? A beast no more.*"
Is this a challenge? Noble challenge of lore?

V. Here I am. Now.
Cold Moon eclipses shortness of days
of deepest, bleakest nights. I hear Vivaldi
and snow winds whistling through secure doors.
By firelight, by starlight, I am reading *Hamlet*,
older, no wiser, to know, ken these words.
Sometimes, I, too, am of two minds, whether
to speak or unravel/hush my weak words.
I follow icy breaths and step outside
to call to the moon - - - I am not yet done this soon.

The more I see this earth, air, fires, waters,
the less I know what turns this cosmos, this one.
So many times, he says goodnight to Man.
My words sound frail when I call out to stars,
"*Good night, sweet prince,*" whether near or far.

Orff's "Carmina Burana-O Fortuna" and Pulsars

I. drums, grave and ponderous,
explode and announce voices
singing ancient words, in moody
mystery like Greek choruses.
compelling and fateful in minor
key. the cosmos weighs on us.

> we sing this song
> from black to blue
> trying to help you know us.
> you see us now
> look for us then
> in farthest years and history

II. *pianissimo,* choral voices
each sing the same notes,
powering the motif, which
is repeated and repeated,
pilgrims marching, echoing destiny.
staccato notes draw us in.

> you see us now
> you see us not
> you're blinded by the darkness
> we shine like stars
> but we're not stars
> yet we appear to flicker

III. the slow tempo produces
a broad sound building
excitement like the rousing
speech of a great king.
the simple melody takes
small but weighted steps.

> we magnetize
> we hypnotize

still we're so small and so faint
faster we spin
age upon age
for us there is no deadline

IV. *forte.* underneath,
woodwinds ground the piece
in constant reminder to hear
the message. strings relay reflection
adding to the building tension.
fire-in-the-head.

we're born of stars
we spin around
shining for you to find us
we pull you in
more than the sun
we're like black widow spiders

V. louder still they chant, brass
lending passion. there is no relief
of suspense in this hypnotic
powerful current of notes
and words, between power
and passion, between light and dark.
we are hooked, nodding for more.

who do you know
who'll help you out
to seek and find lost planets?
tick-tock like clocks
we're all wound up
we'll keep the time precisely

VI. now faster the tempo,
rushing to the finale. When
we speak the notes, the language

is translated. brass and drums
siege the stage not allowing us
to take a breath. you feel
their energy in your blood.
at last, notes, words, light
are bound in one gold-braided chord.

we're here for years
we'll shed more light
before we fade
so you will not flail about
and curse the darkness.

Vollenweider's "Caverna Magica" (1st Track) and Hiking in Sicily

I.
stillness precedes sounds of stumbling
over rocks, wondering voices, then
accented by dripping of water. layered
with drum the theme is played on wired
harp. all echo a far-away
journey and discovery of a cave
by one composer track upon track.

Heavy clouds surround Man
and Woman as they hike along
and ask questions until they
are stopped by a rockslide
that reveals an opening
into darkness. They hear the sound
of water dripping/echoing. They enter
the cavern with fear yet desire.

II.
exotic voices sing out ancient
music. yet now more jazzy
while the harp is more pervasive,
ever reaching, posing questions,
brightening then fading. strange
slippery sounds, picking of guitar,
drumming and ethereal humming
create a sublime sense of awe.
you hear the flutes pulling
the harp along to some secret
vanishing point.

In the profound blackness
winds echo and whistle
waves are so loud, they

cannot hear each other. So
they light their lantern
to right their blindness. Still lost
only seeing their shadows
and shadows of the past,
they must climb up where
a shining lantern reveals
handprints on rough walls
The fire shows stories, beasts,
stick figures running and leaping
that elicits a sense of ancient
past calling out in future words.
Overwhelmed with knowing and awe
they are driven to find a way out.

III.
soprano and alto voices chant
in quick rhythm presenting
a mellow melody that interweaves
oboe, brass, flute, gong and guitar.
all expanding the sound
of relentless harp. voices
and harp fade. there is a pause
and you hear the eerie sound
of leaping then splashing of bubbles
and perhaps the distant
haunting call of a grand whale.

Continuing to rise, ducking crystals
above them, they are drawn by winds
and glimmers of light and they follow.
They hear the sound of seas crashing
on rocks that lead them out
of the cavern. Not thwarted by grueling
paths, they reach the end of the cave.

The end of darkness. Soon they are blinded
by the moon and stars, the beauty
of the breathing world and struggle
to find the words to convey what they
know in the light. At a distance
lamps glow in a village and they
are obliged to tell of what they
had seen and now know, while they
journeyed through the mystical cave.

Eagles' "Hotel California" and Martian Territory

I. chords of two acoustic guitars
and a solo voice introduce the song
boldly and exotically like an owl's
summons from deep woods.
percussion backs the melody while
electric guitars chime in.

> In the cool of the evening on midsummer nights
> When you see fireflies blinking in Thunder Moon's light
> When you see embers of campfires, don't nod off to sleep
> Can't you see that you just might miss the show
> Here you'll find memories you can keep
> Just focus on the red glow
> You'll see Venus near Mars
> From here we see your blue light
> In the swirl of Milky Way stars
> Just peer beyond the darkness and stir up clouds of dust
> Hear us and listen to what we say
> Take a peek if you must

II. refrain is sung
in harmonic chorus layered
with emphasis and chiming of
electric guitars. voices are smooth,
compelling and elegant like sirens
chanting from craggy cliffs.

> We live in the Martian Territory
> Not so far away, not so far away
> We are here to stay
> So much to see in the Martian Territory
> When the sky is clear
> You will find us here.

III. lead guitars strum chords layered
in harmony, repeating hypnotic
phrases that awaken you like sweet waves
of light flickering through a projector
revealing scene after dynamic scene.

> You count us number four in line, come see us anytime
> You measure our temperature, find it too hot, too cold
> You may not breathe our air but you'll find a way
> There's so much to see here
> You'll have no regrets
> Explore our Mt. Olympus, see our old volcanoes
> Walk along sandy beaches beneath our two moons
> We are here in the right place, we think you'll agree
> Come see us soon.

IV. in the refrain the beat
becomes more pronounced
while all voices seem
to echo as if they're tunneling
through a vast passage and announcing
their dynamic presence.

> We live in the Martian Territory
> Not so far away, not so far away
> We are here to stay
> Please get in line for the Martian Territory
> When the path is clear, when the path is clear
> We'll be waiting, dear.

V. subdued guitars and solo
voice revisits until the whole
band plays with intensity,
layering note upon note while
persistent phrases insist their plea.
in the riff, guitars dominate

thoughts more emphatically.
they repeat phrases that seem
to say godspeed and farewell
ending on a high note until it
all fades to a whisper.

No doubt we are different
But we're so much like you
We think like you and unlike so few we can talk till we're blue
We're looking for new friends
We have searched far and wide
So close to us, you're just in our reach

You don't need a ticket
We will just let you in
We have seen your past, present and future, from us you can't hide
You have seen our red glow, that's where you are bound
Pack your bags, catch a ride
Just leave your troubles behind
You'll be safe here underground

Oldfield's "Tubular Bells" (1st Track) and Leonardo

I.
bells herald otherworldly obsessions.
souls, ancient, spirits new, breathe life,
haunting pacing a long road. an endless
counting off. past, present, future.
lightning strikes. flash.

> Borne on rainbows, you,
> a prism, parting seen from unseen,
> always in smooth motion, pace
> heights/depths, striding over grassy
> hills to cool valleys. Facing a world
> in flux. Andante, you journey,
> no time for bird's eye . . .
> crossing bridges, straddling
> art and science, faith and denial.
> Backwards, upside [   ], you cipher
> vast thoughts in minute script
> to chart birds' flight, to map [   ],
> to chase moons, worlds, stars . . .

II.
this dreamy outing tells of wired
emotion and timely logic. piano
keys out a riot of notes. Flash.
art and science mingle, whisked
with red elixir of guitars, mandolin
and bagpipe, *ostinato*, layer upon layer
one clime of strength/beauty
promising time-altered/honored
spirits divine. flash.

> Restless, your aire, not bound
> by fences, risky rivers,

rocky climb or still clocks.
You breathe [   ], noble song
of beauty. You see symbols
in signs. You trace blood
in human hearts, wings
of angels, bones of ages.
Your brush, loaded with smoky
mystery, halos Nature, exalts
Man. your song climbs, folding
edges of space and time . . .

III.
high-minded flute reworks
the driving theme. flash.
tripping heart and soul. flash.
bass guitar answers, *ostinato*,
directing us to spark of stars.
boldly the motif gathers, climbs
in intensity. flash.
it climbs and draws to a higher aire.
one step after another. flash.
one sustained hum sublimes
the glassy vault, revealing
Fifth Element.

With grace, you persist
in your quest to search
for answers to [   ] is the stuff
of life. Then your ears . . .
are assaulted by thunder
of swirling waters, by charges
of hungry, backstabbing
rivals. Your faraway [   ]
are blinded by lightning. Shadow.
Your heart arrested by steel
of stone, by fading color

78

and shortness of time . . .
Though breaths may be labored,
you rise higher, climbing
clouds, looking beyond
the horizon, you raise your head
to attend, sublime trails of stars.

IV.
one pen, one player shows
the way. *fouco*, fury of footsteps
harnessing light of sunrise, mad
piano is tamed by organ to reclaim
our hearts until unearthly shadow
of darkness brews a black storm
over raging waters. soon, it is
blushed and hushed by pastel
clouds spilling visible, invisible
colors of white. chimes resume
that steady climb, *fuoco*, higher
and higher, tripping, spilling
potion of energy, a steady sublime
rush, a hum of vitality and Light.

With shy nobility, you
kick up dust along roads.
Waters may seethe, skies may fall,
wild winds may turn to east,
though you may lose your way,
you are not thwarted. No acid rain
can reign you in. And so, you
draw yourself up, resume
your climb. Higher and higher
with notes, sure, magical
You sublime moons, worlds.
All of this.

V.
bells direct footsteps over hills,
over mount, exploring harness
of Light. whistling advances
a mischievous aura of mystery.
rhythm of bass, *lontano*, treks
beyond, questioning. then it fades,
calendo, beneath a sheath
shimmering stars. treasure is found.

In heat of sunrays, exploring
sunset, you reach beyond
your grasp, mind [   ]
matter, smiling with serene,
ageless . . . mysterious smile.
We are imprinted, graced
by the workings of your life,
the brilliance of your mind.
While you whistle a profound
peace, we cannot leave you . . .
never dust to dust . . . You,
always Alive in our souls.

Light-Years Away Playlist

1. Vivaldi's "Winter"

2. John Williams' "Dance of the Witches"

3. David Garrett's cover of Nirvana's "Teen Spirit"

4. J.S. Bach's "Toccata and Fugue"

5. Puccini's "Le Villi, Opera in 2 Acts, Act II: La Tregenda" (Witches' Sabbath)

6. Mozart's "Requiem"-Excerpts (Kyrie/ Dies Irae)

7. Mendelssohn's "Hebrides" Overture

8. M. Williams' "Classical Gas"/D. Garrett's "Baroque Reinvention"

9. Mozart's "Symphony No. 25 Allegro con Brio"

10. Plain Chants-Gregorian/ Anonymous 4

11. Miles Davis' "Round Midnight"

12. Saint-Saens "Danse Macabre"

13. Wagner's "Siegfrieds's Funeral March"

14. Orrf's "Carmina Barana O Fortuna"

15. Vollenveider's "Caverna Magica" (1st Track)

16. Eagles' "Hotel California"

17. Oldfield's "Tubular Bells" (1st Track)

www.ingramcontent.com/pod-product-compliance
Lightning Source LLC
Chambersburg PA
CBHW070350130626
46556CB00007B/3119